Where is God on Tuesday?

Marlene J. Yeo

Edited by Tara Yeo

This book is dedicated to,

Karen Chitty-Boe,

one of the most beautiful, Christ-like, courageous

women I have ever met, whose life and testimony is

a book that needs to be written.

Endorsements

" *F*or all those people who just 'do the church thing' just to say they do it, and for all those who are serving God but find it hard to get over the hurdles and bumps in the road, "Where Is God on Tuesday" is for you. Ministry is not always a pretty little picture, it's hard, sweaty, dirty work with amazing, life-changing, world-altering results... if you stick with it. It's done with love in mind, just like Jesus would do. Thanks, Marlene, for sharing your heart and what God has put in you to do - for love. God commands us to love the unlovable."

Pastor Bill Wilson
Founder and Senior Pastor
Metro Ministries
Brooklyn, New York

"Relationships will be one of your greatest challenges when you receive an assignment from God. I have observed Pastor Marlene applying God's principles in the most difficult of situations, pushing past the opinions of men to accomplish her Father's will. Through it all she functions with great passion and kindness. Pastor Marlene is most certainly "God's Girl," carrying an apostolic anointing for the 21st century!"

Pastor Raffoul Najem, Senior Pastor
Community Christian Fellowship
Lowell, Massachusetts

"We have the privilege of knowing Marlene as mother, Pastor and friend, and we are two of her greatest fans! In each of these roles we have watched her reveal the character and the nature of Christ. We are provoked and inspired by the life of extraordinary faith, love and compassion that she lives. This book goes beyond rhetoric and theory and cuts to the heart of real life brokenness, pain and hardship and how to find God in the midst of your reality."

Darrell and Bethany Temple
Founders and Directors of Justice House of
Prayer (JHOP)
Boston, Massachusetts

"This book is a celebration of a life that draws the presence of God when Marlene is alone or in front of thousands. She and her "homies" have inspired us to press through the darkest of days. We have had the privilege of watching Marlene's grace as she has faced adversity, allowing God to order her steps and season her words with grace. We look forward to the coming days of walking with CCF Street Church as they continue to break yokes of bondage with humility and grace. Praise God for the victory that accompanies Marlene as she continues to allow herself to be a humble vessel of a Holy God."

Matt and Katy Stevens
Founders of Somebody Cares Baltimore and
Chain Reaction
Baltimore, Maryland

"My friend Pastor Marlene Yeo has been one of the best kept secrets in the body of Christ. She is a woman

of faith, love and compassion. I'm so glad she has decided to write a book that speaks of the journey she has been on. I believe her experiences and wisdom will speak profoundly to you and they will bring hope and healing to your soul. And if you're fortunate, you may just catch the fire that burns deep within Marlene for God's Kingdom! Read with expectancy in your heart!"

Pastor Michael Servello Jr.
Senior Pastor
Redeemer Church
Utica, NY

Contents

Acknowledgements xiii

Forward xvii

Preface: You Really Don't Want to

     Skip This Part! xxi

1. Home is Where the Hurt is 29

2. Thank God for God 34

3. Serving Opens Doors 40

4. God Has a Dream 47

5. Down is Up 52

6. If the Burden is Light,

     How Come My Back Hurts? 58

7. These are Your People God 73

8. When the Mission Becomes Your Master.......84

9. The Good, the Bad and the Ugly.....................97

10. Yah, But…..107

11. He is Good, All the Time 116

12. To Be Continued… 129

Acknowledgements

Before I get started, I want to thank God for the great testimonies and stories He has provided me because of His faithfulness. I never had any intention of writing a book until He spoke to me through several prophetic exhortations that He wanted me to do so.

I also thank God for my husband, Harry, and our three incredible children, Brandon, Bethany and Aaron, as well as their wonderful spouses, Tara, Darrell and Josy. They have blessed Harry and I with seven (to date) of the most beautiful, brilliant and wonderful grandchildren. Because of their love for me, they have encouraged me to pursue my greatest passion in this life: to serve Jesus.

I especially want to thank Bethany and Darrell Temple for their prayer support and the sacrificial giving of their time, energy and talent by serving the ministry of Somebody Cares New England and helping with the launch of Community Christian Fellowship's "Street Church." I couldn't have done it without you. Although you are both missed by the entire staff of CCF, we are all so proud of you and the Justice House of Prayer ministry you have birthed and are directing in Cambridge, Massachusetts.

I also thank God for the wisdom I have received from several special men of God who invested their lives into mentoring me. I am modeling in ministry today what they have taught me. To Pastor Raffoul Najem, Pastor Mike Servello Sr., Pastor Mike Servello Jr. and Pastor Doug Stringer: I know you will receive a reward from the Lord for the fruit in my life and ministry.

My deepest gratitude to the Lord is for the amazing servant leaders of SCNE that have laid down their life to help plant and build Community Christian Fellowship of Haverhill....WOW. I have never served with a more faithful, dedicated, caring group of people in my entire life. Although we are extremely diverse (praise the Lord for that), our love for God, people and the mission, "to take the love and power of Christ to the streets," provides the necessary components for a strong and healthy church.

A special thank you to the servant leaders, Pastor Raffoul Najem, Peggy Foley, John and Sandy Furtado & family, Ed and Michelle Lecuyer & family, Jeff and Letriah Masters & family, Kevin and Reggie Moriarty, George and Connie Plouffe & family, Susan Bradley Quaranta, Kathie Raymond, Suzanne Reynolds and Lori Jane Simmer.

Forward

I n the context of time, there are those who are not content with the mediocre, but emerge as change agents and history makers. Marlene Yeo is one of these. Her passionate pursuit of God and to tangibly express His heart by serving the lowly to the mighty in our world is contagious.

It was with great privilege and anticipation that I read Marlene's book, "Where is God on Tuesday?" There is no doubt that the Lord has gifted her with the skill of a ready writer as she clearly communicates her journey and the Kingdom principles she has learned…often through the crucibles of experience.

These experiences provide a heartfelt visual revelation into the Heartbeat of God for our communities and this generation.

There a those who write from the towers of theory, with all the statistics of information that can give us "brain freeze" or "brain overload". Then, there are the Marlene's of this world who offer us far more than just recognizing the problems of our day. She represents one who contends for authenticity in faith with action, yet offering a practical solution to the societal challenges we face in the world today.

This book, will not only inspire your personal walk and journey, but it will motivate you into greater vision and hopes, expanding your faith beyond your own human capacity. You will revisit promises from the Lord for your own life that may have been forgotten, while raising the bar of expectations.

I am thankful for Marlene's life and ministry. I am proud to have her as part of our Somebody Cares global network of churches, ministries and organizations. She is a true Champion of Faith and Compassion!

Dr. Doug Stringer

Founder/President

Somebody Cares America/International

Turning Point Ministries

Preface

"Where is God on Tuesday?" my friend, Katy Stevens, heard me speak at the Somebody Cares International Summit in Houston, Texas. While sharing during the chapter update for Somebody Cares New England, I made the following statement:

> *Typically, on any given Sunday, the family of God gathers together to enjoy the awesome presence of the Lord. We love it when we are stirred by the prayers of the saints, passionate worship, prophetic words of encourage-*

ment and the relevant message that speaks directly to who we are and what we are going through, Yah God!!! Then Monday comes along and someone asks, "How was service on Sunday?" We say, "It was great," because the excitement we felt the day before is still with us, yet we find it surprisingly difficult to remember the worship songs and inspirational words that had been so moving and profound just one day earlier. By Tuesday, our humanity seems more real to us than His presence and we find ourselves wondering, "Where is God on Tuesday?"

I was sharing in the context that, before breakthroughs, there will always be challenges. Often times, we are challenged beyond our human strength, but if we will trust the Lord and not be moved by our flesh, or "self," we are able to be a part of the wonderful, miraculous things the Lord wants to do through us, around us and for us. This book is about some of the challenges God has allowed to cross my path, and how each challenge became a door of opportunity that He used to bring me to a greater death of "self" and into a greater revelation of Him. Because of His amazing grace, I am not angry about what He has allowed in my life. As Joseph said in Genesis 45:7-8, *"God has sent me before you to preserve posterity for you in the earth and to save your lives by a great deliverance. So it was not you who sent me here, BUT God..."* In addition, Romans 8:28 says, *"God works all things together for good to those who love Him and are called according to His purpose."* He has worked it together for my good because my love for Him was greater than my desire for comfort. I chose to remain while He continued the work, preparing me to receive His promises.

For those of you who have asked, "How do I walk through the Mondays and the Tuesdays and enter into the promises of God, while living in the reality of where I am today?" - I pray this book provides you with some answers to that profound question.

This book is written for those of you who want to make a difference in this crazy world but find yourselves limited in resources, time and skills necessary to accomplish what the Lord has called you to do. It is written for those of you who hope that some day, some *one* will believe in what the Lord has called you to do and will help you accomplish it. If that is you, I have a word of wisdom for you: stop looking for the big somebody to give you the big break, to offer you the big opportunity or the big whatever! Start now by obeying God *right* where you are, using *just* what you have. When you look at the accomplishments, resources and influences that others have, it only produces discouragement, jealousy and fear. It will render you powerless in moving forward, and useless where you are.

I have had the opportunity to walk with some wonderful people who love God, some of whom are mentioned in this book (some names have been changed). Some of them stopped making the choice to abide in His grace until they could enjoy the sweet fruit that is produced out of adversity. If we *really* believe the word of the Lord, then we must be willing to live our lives before Him in the hidden place, even if that means no kudos, no praise, no pay, no glory and no favors, and even when we feel destined to experience defeat, difficulty and disappointment. God is the One who opens doors that no man can shut (Rev. 3:7). What is done and spoken in the dark place will be shouted from the housetop (Luke 12:2-4). Suddenly, one day God will say, "It's time, open the gates, you're passing out of this place and into the new place I have for you. I will go before you and I will lead you in." (Micah 2:13) He is the "breaker" and He will break in to break you out!

We are like the nameless, faceless man that God used in Ecclesiastes 9:15: *"Now there was found in the city a poor wise man, and he by his wisdom delivered the city. Yet no one remembered that same poor man."* We may never receive the credit, fame or fortune in this life. But we must live our lives knowing that in eternity the rewards of faithfulness are meant for those who were faithful with what God gave them. They (whoever "they" are) may never know how the Lord used you, but He knows. God knows every act of kindness, every tear shed for those in need of the Savior, every prayer prayed in faith and every hand extended in love to those in need. He is crazy in love with you and me and He is dancing a happy dance over those who serve Him with a glad heart!

As in the words of Ann Kiemel: "I'm just an ordinary girl with an extraordinary God." This book is about my journey as an ordinary person fulfilling the extraordinary purposes of God in my generation. I have learned to press through the Tuesdays when it feels like God is a galaxy away by trusting that He will do what He has promised and finish what He has started in my life. My prayer for you, as you read this book, is that you will be encouraged to press into His destiny for you, regardless of the obstacles, the trials and the pain.

Before you continue reading, I must warn you that my honesty may offend you and my silly humor may cause you to think I am not doctrinally sound. To the first I say: "Oops!" and to the latter, I say: "Oh well!" Try as I might to behave, I am quite certain some of my personality will leak through the pages of this book. I pray that the testimonies of God's faithfulness written in the pages of this book will encourage you to press past your Tuesdays into the promises of God for your life!

Chapter One

Home is Where the Hurt is

I was raised in a typical American home. Our family attended church on the expected American holidays such as Easter and Christmas Eve. I never owned a Bible or heard anyone in our family talk about God except when the name of Jesus Christ was used as a swear word when someone was angry. Born in 1952 to alcoholic parents, I am the oldest of three children with two younger brothers. Although they loved each other, my parents did not get along. My mother struggled with mental illness and my Dad was a workaholic. Being at work and

away from Mom was a relief for Dad. Their relation-
ship was extremely volatile and very stressful on
all of us. Mom and Dad verbally abused each other
often, which sometimes escalated into physical abuse
that would wake me and my two brothers. Because
of the unrest in our home, my brothers and I had rela-
tional and behavioral issues that would provoke our
parents, both of whom were unskilled in managing
their own negative behavior and emotions. They
would lash out at us verbally and physically. Many
times, we would experience excessive beatings
rather than discipline with instruction. The neglect
and abuse my brothers and I experienced developed
a shame-based character in each of us, causing us to
act out in socially, morally and relationally destruc-
tive lifestyles.

My parents' marriage inevitably ended in divorce
after nineteen years. The painful memories of life
in our family left deep wounds on my self-image. I
have no memory of my parents reading me a book,
playing with me or tucking me into bed. I never felt

protected, celebrated or cared for. My brothers and I have a strong bond and a deep love for each other, of which I believe is a result of what we had to endure growing up. Although we live very different life styles and don't agree about the Lord or the Bible, it has not changed the bond of love and respect we have for one another.

From an early age, I felt uncomfortable in my own skin. I didn't like who I was, what I looked like or my personality. At the core of my being was self- rejection. When I was very young and still in my crib, I repeatedly dreamed about a strange man standing over my bed with a very long, thick rope. He would tie it to one corner of the bedpost and wind it around my bed. I felt like I was being buried alive. Feelings of rejection invaded every part of my life, even my dreams.

Standing or sitting still was a torturous form of punishment to my sanguine personality. My Mom, on the other hand, was a melancholy bookworm who enjoyed quiet and solitude. She would say to me "for god's sake, can't you sit still for one minute?" When the Madagascar movie came out several years back, I thought they had stolen my theme song: "We like to move it, move it."

At the age of twelve, I remember running away from home one night to find refuge at a friend's house. It was then that my friends mixed my first drink and gave me my first cigarette. As the years progressed, drinking became a daily part of my life as a means to self-medicate my emotional pain. I thought drinking gave me a sense of joy, peace and courage, when, in reality, it was opening doors to more confusion, fear, abuse and addiction.

Without a moral compass to guide me, my teenage years continued to spiral out of control. I continually made bad choices. My mentality was like the song lyrics, "all we are is dust in the wind." I didn't care about anything except doing what I wanted, when I wanted and with whom I wanted. As the years passed, I became more self-conscious, self-absorbed and self-centered.

A very dear friend of mine, Janice, continually witnessed to me about God's love for me and that He had sent His Son to demonstrate His love. Oftentimes, I rejected her efforts. I found it difficult to believe that God existed and cared about me. My world of pain was more real to me than God.

Janice was not moved by my rejection and continued to pray for me. One late night in January 1977, while clicking through the channels, I came across a Christian television show. The man hosting the show shared the truth about God's love and invited viewers to pray and accept Jesus as their Lord and Savior. I responded with my whole heart, as tears poured down my cheeks. Finally, I experienced real peace for the first time in my life.

Chapter Two

Thank God for God

After my conversion, and before finding a local church in which I wanted to attend, I traveled to a Catholic charismatic healing service in Boston with some friends from work. It was there that I experienced my first miraculous healing. I had suffered chronic psoriasis on my hands and feet to the point that I avoided exchanging money with a cashier or shaking another's hand because I was so ashamed of the ugliness of my hands. My bloody, cracked, oozing flesh made me feel like a leper. I had been treated with medication and ointments, but they didn't do any good because my condition was neurological in nature. The second morning after the healing service, the skin on my hands and feet was like that of a newborn baby's. It was clean, clear and brand new! My faith in God sky-rocketed to new heights. Not only did He forgive my sins, He saved me from an immoral path of destruction, healed my broken heart, healed my diseased body and jangled nervous system and, better yet, He gave me His joy and peace!

I often wish I could say that suddenly everything changed in my life…but it didn't. It took many years of prayer and counseling from the word of God before I experienced healing of the wounded emotions that were once my constant companion. It is amazing to me how we, the created ones, resist the gift of life and peace that the Creator desires so much to give us. We deceive ourselves into thinking that our life-styles of bondage and sin are lives of freedom and happiness. All I can say is, as I applied the principles of truth found in the word of God and as I chose to remain in that truth through prayer, obedience and the help of the Holy Spirit, He changed EVERY area of my life. I became a new creature in Christ...the old things passed away and all things became new (II Corinthians 5:17). As the children of Israel looked at the serpent Moses lifted up in the wilderness that had bit them, they were healed. Although the enemy's purpose was to destroy my life, the areas of my life that had been wounded are the same areas in which God has anointed me to bring healing to others.

I never had an emotional bond with my mother, but in the last years of her life, I had the privilege of caring for her in my home for almost two years. As difficult as it was, I knew it was an opportunity to share God's love with her. Although she still refused to extend forgiveness to my father, the Lord opened her heart as she asked for forgiveness for the sins of her life. When she died, the only emotion I felt was sadness for her and the painful life she had lived. She had never found happiness. My hope is that she finally let go of her bitterness and forgave my father the night she passed in a nursing home

Although I believe my Dad loved me, he had a difficult time expressing it. He spent most of his life working hard so that our basic needs were met. From the time I was 18 years old, he had had a number of girlfriends, wives and stepchildren. In his elder years, his health failed miserably. It was during that time that we were finally able to connect relationally. During one of my visits with him in Florida, as I gave him a foot soak, I felt in my heart that I should wash his feet and pray for him. He wept as I shared with him how much I loved him and that I knew he had done the best he could to raise us amidst the many difficulties. I offered to pray with him to receive the love of Christ. With great joy, he experienced forgiveness and the peace and presence of God.

Have you ever been angry with God for allowing you to be born into your family, for being mistreated at the job he has provided you, for living next door to a difficult neighbor or for sending you to a church where you have been misunderstood? I can relate, and I am here to tell you, He has a purpose in it all! Jeremiah 1:5 says: *"Before I formed you in the womb I knew you, before you were born I set you apart; I appointed you as a prophet to the nations."* In addition, Romans 8:28 says: *"God works all things together for good, to those who love Him and are called according to His purpose."* He worked it together for my good because my love for Him was greater than my desire for comfort. I chose to remain faithful while He continued His work of preparation in me to receive His promises.

At the time of writing this book, I have walked with the Lord for thirty-three years. I have seen multitudes of people come to the saving knowledge of Christ, experiencing awesome breakthroughs of healing and freedom. The word of God speaks about our journey with Christ as being a daily walk; taking up our cross and denying our "self" (Luke 9:23). Not all continue on the path to holiness and allow the Holy Spirit's work of transformation in their lives. Many allow the difficulties, trials and temptations of life to choke out and scorch the seed of faith (Matthew 13:18-23). It is a difficult journey, one of dying to "self" and choosing His ways and thoughts over our own. Unfortunately, many get discouraged and give up along the way. As my friend Peggy says, "Thank God for God." He paid the highest price by giving the life and blood of His sinless Son in exchange for a depraved, lost humanity and I am forever grateful and amazed that He broke into my prison and captured my heart with His love!

Chapter Three

Serving Opens Doors

As a young believer, I remember attending my first conference and asking the Lord what He wanted me to do to serve Him. Before the end of the weekend, He directed me to Ecclesiastes 9:10, *"What ever your hand finds to do, do it with your might; for there is no work or device or knowledge or wisdom in the grave where you are going."* Many people get stuck in having to know their gift and calling before they begin to serve the Lord. When I read about the gifts of the Holy Spirit, I had a hard time identifying what my particular gifts were. This verse was a welcome relief. It was simple: do what needed to be done with all of my heart.

Although I had heard many teachings about the gifts of the Holy Spirit, it was years before I received personal revelation regarding my own. I am glad the Lord hasn't allowed things to come easily to me. It has taught me to trust and obey Him, even when I don't "get it." It has also taught me to serve Him because of who He is, not because of the gifts He gives.

An elder in the church I was attending once said to me, "It's just a matter of time before you will be in leadership because you take care of God's stuff as if it were your own." Whenever a church clean up was scheduled, I showed up ready to work. When trash was on the floor, I picked it up. When the toilet paper roll was empty, I replaced it. I enjoyed making God's house clean and orderly. Over the years, I have noticed that serving in clean up and prayer are areas in which the least amount of people feel "called."

As my children continued to grow, my service in church grew as well. I served in the nursery, kid's church, youth ministry and VBS. Eventually, when my kids were teenagers, I served as the youth minister for the subsequent ten years. After that, I served as Associate Pastor during their young adult years.

It's wonderful when the Lord works the principle of serving into your life. You don't have to try very hard because serving is a part of who you are and you enjoy doing it because you know that it brings God and others great joy. There are many people who strive to use their spiritual gift(s) on a platform, to be seen by men. They have not learned the principal of serving in the hidden place whereby serving becomes the open door that will make room for their gifts. To quote an old friend of mine, the Big 'O': "You serve your way to your purpose." The little Yeo (that's me) would add, "And when you find your purpose, keep serving."

I was powerfully impacted by a message Pastor Bill Wilson of Metro Ministries preached regarding I Chronicles 13 and 15. In this passage, David chose the home of Obed-Edom to keep the ark of the presence of God for three months. Obed-Edom was a servant in the house of the Lord; he did whatever needed to be done. Servants are the keepers of the ark of His presence. My heart's cry is, "Lord, let us be carriers of Your presence. Let Your peace and power be real to a lost and dying world. Let them see Christ living in us when we choose to not allow disappointments, pain and difficulties to render us useless, but that, through Your grace, we would rise above the difficulties to become better skilled and more useful."

The Son of Man was the greatest Servant Leader of humanity. He came not to be served, but to serve. *"So when He had washed their feet, taken His garments, and sat down again, He said to them, 'Do you know what I have done to you? You call Me Teacher and Lord, and you say well, for so I am. If I then, your Lord and Teacher, have washed your feet, you also ought to wash one another's feet. For I have given you an example, that you should do as I have done to you. Most assuredly, I say to you, a servant is not greater than his master; nor is he who is sent greater than he who sent him. If you know these things, blessed are you if you do them.'"* (John 13:12-17).

Over the years many have asked, "How is it that you have been able to step into the prophetic promises God has given you? Many have a calling but few have actually stepped into their destiny." The answer is very simple yet very difficult:

- **Pray**—Pray and keep on praying. Choose not to be controlled by what is and believe what God says.
- **Obey**—Do whatever the Lord speaks to you from His Word. Just do it! So, you're not so skilled, so great or even so good...so what, just do it!
- **Remain**—Regardless of the obstacles and challenges, stay put; don't run.
- **Trust**—Trust the Lord instead of the other voices screaming, "Why can't you just be normal? Why do you care so much? If you

were really called to do this, wouldn't it be easier?"

- **Press**—Keep pushing, don't give in and never give up! Even after having done all you know to do....stand! He loves to reveal Himself through impossible situations.

- **Character**—It isn't what men say *about* you, it's what angels *know* about you. To God and thine own self be true. Everyone will have an opinion about you. One day, they call you a hero; the next day, you're a zero. Don't let public opinion move you. Don't take credit for what works or blame for what doesn't. Let success and failure be a tool to mold you into Christ-likeness.

- **Honor**—Give credit where credit is due. Don't act smarter than you are. Honor those whom God places in your life that make you look good.

- **Rest**—Take time out to rest along the way to be renewed and refreshed. It may take five,

45

ten, twenty or even thirty years for you see the fruit of your labors. You're in it for the long haul, until death do us part. There is no plan B. Sometimes we end up trying too hard, but I have found that the more I rest in Him, the better things work out.

- **Give Him thanks in, for and through all things**—It keeps you out of the prison house of self-pity and keeps your eyes fixed on the prize!

Chapter 4

God Has a Dream

O ften, I have prayed according to Joel 2:28, asking that God would give me dreams and visions. It was not until August 1998, while attending a compassion conference in Utica, New York at Mt. Zion Ministries (now renamed Redeemer Church), that I realized God has dreams. He revealed to me that He dreams of a church that would tell the whole world of His love, by demonstrating His love one to another, and being the tangible expression of His compassion and mercy to others.

His heart for His kids is that they not only get along, but that they actually love one another. John 13: 34-35 says, *"A new commandment I give to you, that you love one another as I have loved you, that you also love one another. By this all will know that you are My disciples, if you have love for one another."*

None of us can reach the "whole world" but we can begin with our own family, neighborhood, school, job and city. His dream is that His bride, the church, would be the manifestation of His love, demonstrated in each part of the world in which we live (Matt. 22:37-39).

Pastor Harold Caballeros of Almolonga, Guatemala was one of the guest speakers at the Compassion Conference in Utica, New York. I had first heard his testimony about how the Lord brought transformation to his city on the first *Transformation* DVD produced by Sentinel Group (www.glowtorch. org). At the conference, the Lord gripped my heart. For three days, my nose was in the carpet repenting for not having His heart for the people. I cried out to Him that he would send me wherever He wanted me to go.

Jesus said the two great commandments are to love the Lord with all your heart and to love your neighbor as yourself: *"That they all may be one, as You, Father, are in Me, and I in You; that they also may be one in Us, that the world may believe that You sent Me"* (John 17:21). Who is my neighbor, you ask? Why, it's your neighbor! The person who is standing, sitting, eating, sleeping, working or walking next to you right now. God wants to answer the prayer Jesus prayed for His disciples. He is waiting for us to choose to walk in love. How His heart is grieved when His children contend and fight with one another. We have been a poor witness to the world. It is time to build bridges, put aside foolish pride, humble ourselves, and reach out to our brothers and sisters. We *must* come together because of Jesus and love our cities together for the sake of the lost.

God dreams of a day when the Church returns to it's calling as a house of prayer. Isaiah 56:7 and

Mark 11:17 says, *"My house shall be called a house of prayer for all nations."* The thought of starting a house of prayer never entered my mind until I climbed the stairs of the Moravian prayer tower in Germany. During a ten day trip to Europe with my brother, Marland, and my daughter, Bethany, I spent two days in Herrnhut, Germany where Count Zinzendorf had spent His life as a compassion prayer missionary. It was there that an outpouring of the Holy Spirit began a 24/7, prayer movement that endured for over 100 years. As I stood at the top of this tower, looking out across the beautiful land of Germany, I felt the presence of the Lord and began to sob for America. My heart cried out, "Lord, please birth 24/7 prayer in every city across America. Bring the church of Jesus Christ together to pray for the well being of her cities. America needs a move of the Holy Spirit once again."

When I returned home from Germany, I gathered my leadership staff together and shared the call I felt from the Lord to birth a Haverhill House of Prayer.

We fasted and prayed for 21 days, seeking the Lord for His anointing to launch it. At the end of the three weeks, we invited Jeff Marks, an apostolic prayer intercessor and father in the faith. Jeff has labored in prayer for New England, America and the nations for decades. November 2007 marked the beginning of Monday through Saturday prayer. The scheduled prayer set times can be found on www.somebody-caresne.org. People from all denominations, many states and other nations have served in this humble house of prayer over the last several years. We are expecting the Lord to continue to add faithful inter-cessors who will help expand the prayer set times. We know the Lord will build His house of prayer, as we faithfully serve Him where we are with what we have.

Chapter Five

Down is Up

After my powerful encounter with the Lord in Utica, New York, I thought I would then be catapulted into my destiny. Instead, after receiving revelation of His dream, I plummeted to the depths of despair. I refer to this season in my life as one of my many trips into the bowels of hell. Until this point, my life in ministry had been pretty normal, sane and predictable.

During this time, my home, my relationships, my ministry and my finances suffered, what I considered to be, unbearable losses. The Lord used this painful period of about three years to transition me out of the church in which I had been serving for twenty years. I had never been through an experience of brokenness in ministry of this magnitude before, and I have to say, I did not handle the confusing, painful circumstances with great skill or emotional maturity.

When Joseph received his dreams from God, the first place he experienced the greatest challenge was his closest relationships. It is evident from scripture and my own experience, that misunderstanding, jealousy and fear are assigned to escort you to your new assignments from God. In addition to the emotional upheaval of losing the comforts of home, everything Joseph knew was taken from him. Although he served where God allowed him to go, he was accused of wrongdoing, even though he was innocent. It is one thing to read about the life of Joseph, but it is another to walk a mile in his moccasin and gain understanding about the process the Lord wants to bring us through. After receiving revelation from His Word, you will be baptized in the furnace of affliction. If your responses are correct, you will not only survive the painful circumstances, but you will learn to thrive in spite of them, ultimately arriving at the joy of seeing the promise come to pass (Genesis: 37-50).

As we advance forward into our destiny, we often find ourselves in a downward spiral. In my spiral downward, I experienced emotions of intense fear and great confusion. My carnal thoughts were, "I must have done something terribly wrong." "If this is how God treats His favorites, how do I get off His favorites list?" It felt as though the gods were angry with me and trying to kill me (I know there is only one God; pardon my personality leaking through)!

It is during times of testing that it feels like God is distant and silent, withholding revelation and under-standing of what is happening. I have learned to embrace those dark times as a crucible that God uses to reveal the thoughts and intents of my heart, as He prepares me to receive what He has promised. Psalm 12:6 says, "*The words of the Lord are pure words, like silver tried in a furnace of earth, purified seven times."* In preparing us to receive His promises, He allows our faith to be tried in the furnace of the earth; the deepest place of our soul. We don't know who we really are or what is lodged deep inside of us. Only the Lord knows the secrets of the heart.

Jesus allowed Peter to walk through the pain of denying Him, exposing Peter's heart to himself. Jesus prayed that Peter would strengthen the brethren once he was restored. Peter went from being "the one who knew everything," to "the one who knew nothing," and the Lord knowing everything (Matthew 26:35; John 21:17). Those places in us must be revealed and healed so that we will be ready and able to enter into our destiny.

Pastor Bill Wilson ministered to our church and encouraged us with the story about the tribe of Benjamin in Judges 20:15-16. He shared with us that, even though we may have been wounded in previous battles, God can still use us and that the difficult battles we think we might have lost, only serve to strengthen us for future battles. In Judges 20:15-16, the tribe of Benjamin consisted of an army of 700 select, left-handed warriors. Left-handed people were outcasts. They were considered to be undesirables, even despite the fact that they were extremely skilled with their left hands. Each one of them could sling a stone at a hair's breadth and not miss their target. Where do 700 left-handed men of war come from? Could it be that they had been in previous battles and suffered the loss of their right hands? Did this disability cause them to retrain their left hands? The Bible is full of stories about fragile, weak human beings; men, women and young ones who were the least, the last and the lost. God delights in choosing them to accomplish His purposes. It is the wounded ones who have been healed that God uses as secret weapons to break through enemy lines with His love!

Has there ever been a time in your life when you received a dream or a word from God revealing that which He has called you to do, sparking a burning desire within you to serve Him? Did the Lord allow testing and pain to enter your life, causing you to roll over and go to sleep as the disciples did in the garden? It is time to shake off the slumber of pain and discouragement, just as Paul shook the serpent off his arm at the coal fire in Malta. As you surrender to God, He will take the horrible experiences of your life and wash them with His blood, making you better, not bitter. It's time to give it up, give it over and give in to His process of perfecting you. Once you do, you will be amazed as the Lord does miracles in you, for you, around you and through you!

Chapter Six

If the Burden is Light, How Come My Back Hurts?

Matthew 11:30: "For My yoke is easy and My burden is light."

I always thought receiving a burden from the Lord should be easy, as in "a piece of cake" like "no sweat." Oh my, I had no clue. According to Webster's dictionary, burden is defined as, "that which is borne with difficulty; to load heavily; to load oppressively; to trouble." Basically, it is a difficult duty, requiring effort. When I received the Lord's burden for my life, to serve as a prayer compassion missionary to Haverhill, Massachusetts, I gained a new understanding of the term "blood, sweat and tears."

Part of my assignment has been to bring reform to the Christian community mindset. I have found there is a false ideology regarding prayer and missions in the western church. It is a stronghold in the mind and heart of many believers. You can hear the mindset woven throughout most conversations regarding prayer and missions. It sounds something like this, "Not everyone is called to pray for their cities. Missions is for those nations that need it and America is not one of those nations. We are already a Christian nation with access to education, doctors and welfare."

Little did I know, after returning home from the Compassion Conference in 1998, *everything* was about to change. At the time, I was serving as the Youth Minister in a local church and immediately began to share the burden God had given me with church leadership. His heart for those right here on the streets of America. Acts 1:8 says, *"….you will be My witnesses first in Jerusalem, then Judea, Samaria and the uttermost."* God had called me to my Jerusalem: Haverhill, Massachusetts. I announced to the youth and leadership staff, "We will never return to business as usual, the ministry will now be missions focused." Subsequently, we began an intensive three-month training program to teach the young people and leaders to be missionaries to their schools, their neighborhood and to those on the streets of Haverhill.

In July 1999, we organized our first Block Party in downtown Haverhill at GAR Park. I invited a youth minister friend of mine from Michigan and he brought his leadership staff, youth ministry team, band, and drama team of about thirty people. We experienced an amazing day of music, ministry, food, and fun. We fed hundreds of people, including single moms, children, youth, elderly, homeless and the distressed of the city. My heart was gripped by the desperation I saw in their eyes. And at the same time,

I was blessed by their beautiful smiles and expressions of gratitude, thankful God had used us to touch their lives. I knew from that moment the Lord had called me not to just "do" outreaches, but to "be" the outreach by which God could draw the people whom He wanted us to show His love and kindness. That December, the youth prepared for their next opportunity to share the love of Jesus with people in distress. Instead of participating in a Yankee swap with one another, we planned a Christmas party for the homeless. I challenged the youth to save their money and consider asking their parents for up to half of the money they would normally spend on gifts so they could buy new gifts for the homeless to be given out on Christmas Day.

Although the outreach was presented as an option for those youth and their families that wanted to be involved it was a challenging time for all. As the time came closer mindsets, fears and insecurities were exposed. Some parents felt it was a disruption to the "family tradition" with their child involved in serving at an outreach on Christmas Day. Some were afraid their kids would be in danger. After all, the homeless were "dangerous people." The saddest mindset of all was "How can you do this to us? This is a holy day for families." My response to them was, "What would Jesus be found doing on Christmas Day? The greatest gift we could give Him is to share His love with the forgotten ones."

On Christmas Day, approximately twelve youth and eight adults went to the homeless shelter and experienced something that NONE of us had experienced before. The presence of Jesus was tangible. There were tears of joy shed by all who were present as we shared a meal, the love of Christ, the good news of the gospel and gifts for each individual. Just one day earlier, a woman who was known to be the worst drunk in Haverhill, tried to strangle a young black man who was a known drug user. He had punched her in the face when trying to defend himself. His neck was a raw, bloody mess, and the woman's face looked like a raccoon. After I shared about the greatest Christmas gift of all, Jesus, the woman received His love and forgiveness. Immediately, she went to the man she had tried to strangle the previous day, and they wept together exchanging forgiveness with one another.

One father, Chuck Benedict, brought his teen-agers to protect them from the "evil people" in the shelter. As they were leaving, he said to me, "This was the best Christmas I have ever had in my life! I experienced what Christmas is all about. It's about giving the love of Christ freely to those He died for. I came here thinking I needed to protect my kids, but God's plan was to wreck my heart with His compassion for the people who need His love."

Since our first Christmas Day outreach in 1999, we have been serving breakfast and lunch to the community on all of the national holidays, including Thanksgiving, Christmas and New Years Day. During our holiday outreaches, from 7:00am-4:00pm, we provide day shelter, clothing, and a tractor trailer truckload of groceries and personal care products, music, prizes and most importantly, an atmosphere of love and compassion.

Several hundred people over the years have said, "If it wasn't for Somebody Cares, I would have no one to be with during the holidays. You are my family, and being here with all of you is what I look forward to every year." Many of the addicts and alcoholics have thanked us for giving them a reason not to use that day, saying, "I used to have to get wasted to escape the loneliness I felt on the holidays. Thanks for giving me a reason to be sober!"

The pain and difficulty these precious people endure is beyond words. Yes, many of them have made bad choices that have caused them to end up in their current state of despair, however, most of them have been sinned against by others when they were small children and teenagers, causing them to become emotionally crippled beyond human repair. Short of a miracle, there is no hope for them to change the lifestyles they live in. I know nothing is impossible with God, because of the miracles Christ has done in my life,! I have the faith to believe that He is able to rescue those in the "gutter most" and raise them up to the "uttermost", because of my own personal experiences.

Although being called to the mission of loving people who are the least, the last and the lost is challenging, it has also been a great joy and a delight to my heart. I remember seeing one man at our Christmas Day outreach, I will call Jim. He was looking over the gift table where our guest's could choose and wrap a gift for a loved one as well as receive a gift from Somebody Cares for themselves. He was distressed, depressed, homeless and lonely. His remark to me was, "Nobody cares about me on Christmas Day or any other day!" I was able to encourage him that the very reason we were there offering a day of shelter, food, fun, prayer and resources, was because of Jesus' great love for him. I shared with him that *everything* we did on that day was God demonstrating His love through us just for him. His eyes filled with tears as we looked for his gift. At the end of the day he came to me and said, "I have never felt what I experienced here today. You gave me the gift of love and peace." That night, Jim went back to the shelter knowing that Jesus loved him.

That is the reward for the blood, sweat and tears. When you get to be the donkey God uses to carry His presence into your "Jerusalem," you have the privilege of watching Him reveal His love to hurting people only to see them touched by His love!

In June of 2002, I met a very special man named Pastor Doug Stringer. A mutual friend of ours, Helena Wang, had shared Doug's story with me and encouraged me to meet him. When Doug was twenty-five years old, he began taking a group of Christian young people onto the streets of Houston, Texas as the bars were closing. Doug and his group would pass out "Somebody Cares" business cards with a 24-hour phone number to the runaways, addicts, prostitutes and anyone in distress. Today, the ministry of Somebody Cares (www.somebodycares.org) serves multiple cities throughout America and several nations. The Lord is using Somebody Cares as first responders in disasters across the globe.

Helena had tried to arrange a conversation between Doug and I on several occasions, but I was pretty good at dodging them. Because I was comparing the magnitude of Doug's ministry to the little outreaches I was doing in Haverhill, I felt extremely insecure and thought I would be wasting his time. Despite my attempts to avoid the inevitable, the Lord cornered me, and I ended up having lunch with Doug, Helena and my daughter, Bethany.

As I shared with Doug my passion for Jesus and the compassion He had put in my heart for the people, tears flooded my salad, making it nearly impossible to eat. I explained how my heart became burdened for the people after watching the *Transformation* video; something happened to me that couldn't be explained. I apologized for being so emotional and explained that I often got blubbery when sharing my passion. As Doug listened intently, looking at me wide-eyed, I thought to myself, "This guy thinks I am a cuckoo head." Surprisingly, his response was very comforting. In his very calm, Asian manner, he put my blubbering emotions into words and said, "You are carrying a burden from the Lord for your city. He has raised you up as a woman of peace. I would like to come to your city and meet the people you serve."

In November of 2002, Doug paid his own way to come to Massachusetts where he ministered in two churches and shared the vision of Somebody Cares with five area pastors. During his visit, we walked the streets of Haverhill and I introduced him to my "homies" at the day shelter. Doug said he felt there was a DNA for city transformation here in the city and he said, "As you wash the feet of the poor, it touches the heart of the Father and releases the blessing of His presence. His presence is what will transforms lives."

I then brought Doug to the abandoned campus, formerly Bradford College, that was for sale at the time. Originally, it had been founded as a private Christian school.

One of the first missionaries to leave American soil, Ann Haseltine, had graduated from Bradford College. As Doug stood there on the property, he said, "I believe the Lord wants to re-dig the wells here on this campus and send out missionaries once again from this place that will touch the four corners of the world. Gather the intercessors together and pray it through and watch what the Lord will do!" We did just that. We petitioned intercessors throughout New England and began to walk the property, calling those things that were not as though they were. Not only did we pray regularly on campus, we did prayer walks throughout the city as the Lord revealed where He wanted us to go.

By March 2003, Somebody Cares New England was incorporated and licensed under the covering of Somebody Cares America. The founder, Dr. Stringer is an honorary board member of the New England chapter.. SCNE is not a para-church organization that facilitates humanitarian deeds. It is a living organism made up of people who are *praying* for the transformation of lives and cities, while *caring* and meeting practical needs and *sharing* the good news of God's love. Prior to becoming a Somebody Cares Chapter, we did outreaches and were a blessing to the people we served, but since become a chapter, we have become a relational net in five cities, joining hands with over twelve denominations and three synagogues, participating in holiday outreaches and block parties with hundreds of volunteers that serve from all walks of life.

When you put your hand to the plow, it stirs up a hornet's nest in the spiritual realm. The enemy doesn't care how much you know, he's concerned with you stepping out in faith and putting into practice what you know. Nehemiah 4:1 says, *"But it so happened, when Sanballat heard that we were rebuilding the wall, that he was furious and very indignant, and mocked the Jews."* The enemy stirred up contention, strife, gossip and jealousy among area churches and pastors creating such calamity and confusion that I found myself emotionally wrestling with the idea of no longer being a part of Somebody Cares (never mind interceding for the re-digging of the missions well). The backlash of accusation and slander continued for several years. One pastor spoke publicly opposing the ministry of Somebody Cares and told a number of people he spoke to not to get involved with SCNE because I was a woman in rebellion.

Several years ago, I was invited to lead the prayer segment for "Unity in the Church" for the National Day of Prayer (NDP). When another pastor in the city found out I was scheduled to speak, he told the NDP Coordinator to remove me because of the accusations he had heard about me. She was mortified when she called to un-invite me. I humbled myself that day and went to pray for the city with my brothers and sisters in Christ, determined not to allow false accusations to deter me.

The Lord has a way of turning things around. This past year, Somebody Cares New England was asked to co-chair the NDP with Common Ground Ministries. The same woman who had the difficult job of telling me I couldn't participate several years earlier, came up to me to express her gratitude to the Lord for vindicating me and said, "I am so sorry. I knew you were all about unity, but I couldn't defend you and I am so glad the Lord did!" I had the joy of telling her how God used it to do a work of humility in me, and I didn't blame her or her pastor because my steps are ordered of the Lord!

Chapter Seven

These are Your People God

As a minister of reconciliation, many times my heart has sobbed for the people I serve in the inner city as well as the people of God who already have knowledge of the word of the Lord. At times, I have found myself annoyed with God for not doing what I think He should be doing to bring about justice for those I serve, as well as for myself. Time and time again, I have to remind myself: these are God's people, not mine. I giggle when I think about the conversation between God and Moses regarding the children of Israel. I'll paraphrase like this:

Moses: "God, do something with Your people!"
God: "Moses, get down off the mountain and do something with your people!"

When the outreaches in Haverhill first began, there was tremendous excitement in the church I was attending at the time.. It was the "new thing" that got everyone revved up. It was fun and exciting. Often times, when a ministry is birthed, like with a new baby, everyone feels "called" to join what's happening, when in reality, they are just coming to check it out.

Not everyone feels "called" to take care of the night feedings or change the messy diapers. The majority want to show up to serve on the day of the party, well after the hard work of raising funds, gathering resources has taken place. When the party is over, volunteers disappear rather quickly because few feel called to the ministry of "clean up." After all, they don't want to get their party pants dirty!

During the second year of facilitating outreaches in Haverhill, concerns arose in my home church among the leadership staff that too many church members were serving the inner city mission instead of serving in areas of ministry within the church. Discussions took place about how SCNE was causing a division (two different visions) within the church body because I was drawing church members away from the mission statement of the church: to build a "Charismatic Family Church." Instead, church leadership felt it was beginning to look more like an "Inner City Missions Church."

The city of Haverhill was not only half an hour away from the little, rural church I was attending; it was located across the border in another state. We were given the use of a 15-passenger van to transport the people from Haverhill to our church services each Sunday. It created a bit of a problem. Inner city issues were now present in a white, rural church. What was God thinking?

I found myself in the middle of a very difficult situation. I loved my home church and believed in submitting to its leadership, yet I was leading a mission that seemed to be creating problems for the church, as well as myself. I would vent to God about how unfair it was; after all, I didn't sign up for this, He had drafted me. I told God that He would need to find another donkey to carry His burden for the city. It was messing up my theology on submission to authority and causing distress for everyone around me.

Little by little, I began to spend less time serving in the city. The prayer walks were no longer several times a week, the visits to the homeless day shelter (run by Community Action) became less frequent. I was embarrassed and ashamed that my home church did not feel called to be a part of what God had called me to do. Somewhere in my heart, I had made a decision to back out on God to try to resume a normal life (if that was even possible).

After about six weeks of dealing with all of the "brew-ha- ha," I became exhausted and confused and found myself in a state of numbness. I decided to escape for a weekend conference in Connecticut, hoping to find some relief and to be able to chill out. I was having a wonderful time worshiping the Lord when, suddenly, I saw a picture of the Good Samaritan caring for a wounded man on the big projection screen. I fell apart emotionally, hitting the floor in a puddle of tears. I sobbed, "God, *please*, I can't do this. It's not working and I am not the right one. Find another donkey. I don't have the support of my church; they just don't get me. I can't make them understand and You don't seem to be doing anything about it. What other choice do I have? I have to quit." All of a sudden, not expecting to hear God's voice, He speaks to my heart loud and clear: "Get your eyes off the people. Get your eyes on Me and I will feed a city through you."

Instantly, I felt conviction for pulling away from the people that I had grown to love and for neglecting to pray for the city.

After a long conversation with God, I got up, blew my beak, washed my face and decided to call Pat Dennehey at the Drop-In Center. Pat is the director of the homeless day center in Haverhill. On numerous occasions, I had the opportunity of sharing Jesus with her. Although she doesn't profess to be a Christian, she considers herself to be spiritual, having had spiritual experiences of all kinds. Jesus is not "her thing." Pat and I have a great relationship. Because we share a love for the people in the city, we have a great respect for one another and work very well together. I blubbered to her on the phone, "Pat, please forgive me for not coming to the Drop-In these last six weeks. I have been backing off from the mission. It has been too difficult. I don't have the support I used to have, and the volunteers, resources and finances just aren't there anymore. I am so embarrassed and ashamed. I have let you and the people at the Drop-In down." Pat's response absolutely shocked me. She scolded me in a good, godly way. She said, "Marlene Yeo, it isn't the volunteers, the coats, the boots or the food that you give that matters to these people; it's the love. They know you love them and care about them. You put your arms around people who smell like urine, some of whom are HIV positive. For some of them, your hug is the only one they get. You, of all people, should know it's about the love, not what you give them. You give them yourself and they love you!"

Needless to say, I was back to being the willing donkey. I said to God, "Ok, I'm in. I repent for being like Jonah and trying to run. Even if I only have three dollars, I will buy three hot dogs and feed three people. I am willing to do whatever You want, and God, please don't ever let me forget that "it's all about the love.""

Shortly after coming to that resolution, I received prophetic words from three different people who had never met me before. The condensed version is as follows:

- The leadership in your current church does not understand the call of God on your life for inner city ministry.
- The Lord is going to place you in a church that understands that "City Church" is composed of many churches pastoring the city together.

- God is going to use your husband to help you make the transition. Don't worry, he is going to be alright.
- God is placing you under an apostolic leader that will receive you and release you into the call of God on your life.
- The Lord wants to promote you because you have been loyal and faithful under those whom you have served.
- God is sending you to the dream center in L.A. because He wants you to receive a vision. He wants you to dream big because He desires to use you to build a center in your city.

It's amazing to me how, once you submit to the will of God, He will give you the confirmation and affirmation you need to be able to face the challenges and overcome the obstacles. II Peter 1:19 says, *"And so we have the prophetic word confirmed, which you do well to heed as a light that shines in a dark place, until the day dawns and the morning star rises in your hearts"* and I Timothy 6:12 says, *"Fight the good fight of faith, lay hold on eternal life, to which you were also called and have confessed the good confession in the presence of many witnesses."*

The Bible calls it a *good* fight, which is interesting terminology to me. Fighting to me was never a good thing; I would avoid it at all cost. But God wanted to fashion me as a strong and courageous weapon of His love by teaching me to be skilled at fighting the good fight of faith as described in Psalm 18:29-33: *"For by You I can run against a troop, By my God I can leap over a wall. As for God, His way is perfect; the word of the LORD is proven; He is a shield to all who trust in Him. For who is God, except the LORD? And who is a rock, except our God? It is God who arms me with strength, and makes my way perfect. He makes my feet like the feet of deer, and sets me on my high places."*

I have come to believe that God picks my fights because He knows the outcome and trusts that what He has invested in me is "enough." His intentions for me are always good, believing that I will have a greater revelation of who He is in the end. Job 1:8 says, *"Then the LORD said to Satan, "Have you considered My servant Job, that there is none like him on the earth, a blameless and upright man, one who fears God and shuns evil?"*

Biblically, one can clearly see that God chooses the opponents for the fight - which are either his adversaries, his people or both. The sooner we come to grips with God's means, the sooner we will learn God's ways, which, in turn, plants us in the center of God's will. *"I have heard of You by the hearing of the ear, but now my eye sees You"* (Job 42:5).

My intention in this chapter is not to give a negative view of the Church or God's people, but to prepare you for the reality that you will have to overcome giants in order to step into your destiny. I believe a wrong response to the "giants" is one of the reasons that roots of bitterness and unforgiveness find a place in the hearts of believers. It comes down to one question: When our heart is pierced, will we bleed forgiveness and respond to injustice like Jesus did when he said, *"Father forgive them for they know not what they do"* (Luke 23:34). Many of us have yet to understand the cross and the fact that we have no right to be offended. The path to the promises of God is narrow, indeed.

Chapter Eight

When the Mission Becomes
Your Master

My friend, this chapter is of most importance because it exposes how the mission God has called you to accomplish can actually exalt itself above the Lord of the mission. I have watched many anointed, gifted Christians not finish well because of this very subtle strategy of the enemy. It feeds the desires of the human flesh and will ensnare you. It is extremely lethal and has the potential to destroy you, your family and the mission itself. A few tell tale signs that this deadly enemy is taking over your life: exhaustion, burnout, fear, insecurity, control, manipulation, lying, cheating, exaggeration, out-bursts, anger, judgments, accusations, defensiveness, hiding, compromise and blame.

You may be thinking to yourself, "How does the enemy gain such access in one's life and ministry?" The answer is very simple: we give him the authority to do so. When we cross the boundaries that God has set for us, we end up being driven by the mission instead of being led by the Lord. The human soul wants to be number one, wants to be right, and wants its own way. It boils down to one word, pride, and the human soul is full of it!

King Saul was a man chosen by God to be the king of Israel. He was a tall, handsome man and the Lord said, *"There is no one in all of Israel like him"* (I Samuel 10:24). When Saul was approached by Samuel regarding God's choice, Saul responded in humility saying, *"I am of the smallest of the tribes in Israel, and my family is the least of all the families of the tribe of Benjamin, why then do you speak to me like this?"* (I Samuel 9:21)

It's amazing how a position of authority can change a person. By the end of Saul's life God said, *"I greatly regret that I have set up Saul as king, for he has turned back from following Me, and has not performed My commandments."* (I Samuel 15:11) Saul's heart had turned away from the Lord. He allowed the mission of being king to become his master, rather than the Lord. His life and mission plunged into a downward spiral when he chose to disobey God. He relied on his own wisdom and performed a priestly duty without having God's authority to do. He cared more about being honored publicly by the prophet of the Lord than repenting for his foolish behavior. Saul became jealous of his son Jonathan's relationship with David, because of the next generation leader's double portion anointing. He relied on his own strength and armor instead of the Lord's, and he allowed God's enemies to taunt His people.

When Samuel confronted Saul for his sinful disobedience, he not only denied it, but he deceived himself into thinking that he had actually obeyed. I Samuel 15:20 says, *"And Saul said to Samuel, 'But I have obeyed the voice of the LORD, and gone on the mission on which the LORD sent me, and brought back Agag king of Amalek; I have utterly destroyed the Amalekites.'"* Throughout Saul's life, you can trace the places he chose his mission above his Master. His position of authority was more important to him than his obedience. He misused his anointing and, ultimately, his life ended in defeat. He did not finish well.

It is a sad day when a Christian forgets that their anointing is a gift from God to equip them for the mission they have been called to accomplish. We *must* respect the anointing and honor the Lord with it in all that we do. The authority and power that comes with the anointing is entrusted to us and equips us for the purpose of representing Him well before the people we serve. It is easy to forget what we were like before the Lord graced us with the anointing of His Holy Spirit. Like Jesus, we receive anointing from the Spirit of God because we are sent on God's mission (Luke 4: 1-4). I have listed several safeguards that prevent the mission from becoming your master:

- Foster accountability relationships that will speak truth into your life. I have been blessed to have strong apostolic leaders in my life who are not afraid to instruct, rebuke and correct me. Without truth-speakers, we become vulnerable and weak. When our words, attitudes and behavior are not lining up with the character of Christ, we need a reality check from those who love us more than they love our approval.

- Help others to succeed in what God has called them to do and celebrate with them when they experience success in their lives and/or ministry.

- Keep a "kingdom mentality" in the forefront of your mind and heart ALWAYS. You and I are

His ambassadors. We must never forget that He is the King of His kingdom. The tendency to think "we are the only ones" was in the disciples thinking, and it is in the fiber of the church today. In Mark 9:38-40, John said, *"Teacher, we saw someone who does not follow us casting out demons in Your name, and we forbade him because he does not follow us."* But Jesus said to him, *"Do not forbid him, for no one who works a miracle in My name can soon afterward speak evil of Me for he who is not against us is on our side."*

- Schedule time away from ministry - this will not happen without a fight. Everything within you may scream "Don't do it! The ministry will suffer. People will not handle things like I do!" Do it anyway. If things fall apart, it will only reveal that the foundation was not of Christ. The ministry may suffer loss, but to that I say: oh well, in the kingdom of God, loss is gain. Time away exposes the reality of where you and others need to grow and mature. You have to let others feel the weight of what you carry so they will understand how to come along-side you to better serve in the mission with you. If not, you will always be the one telling people what to do, rather than allowing them to gain the understanding for themselves. I have a saying: "When God is moving it reveals His glory, when He isn't, it reveals our gory." When there is movement, there is excitement. When there is inactivity, we come face to face with ourselves.

- Raise up those whom God has sent to do the mission with you. At some point, the next generation of leaders will be the legacy you leave behind to continue the assignment God gave you to do. Create a platform for them that they may finish well. Show them how to do the mission through the following steps:
    - Model what to do
    - Teach and train how to do it

- Have them do it with you
- Let them do it without you
- Be available as they grow in their ability to manage the ministry well

Sustaining healthy relationships will be one of your greatest challenges when you receive an assignment from God. Some of your closest family members and friends may *never* "get you." In fact, they may be the very ones who oppose you the most. It is not your job to strive to convince them, it is your job to live before them in such a way that you are honoring the Lord while continuing to love them.

There are two references that helped me navigate the relational landmines which accompany life in ministry. In I Samuel 25, David sent his men to ask Nabal for his favor as well as food and drink for the feast day. Nabal's response to the king was not noble. Luckily, Nabal's wife, Abigail, was a woman of great wisdom. She chose to honor King David by being hospitable, and in doing so, her family was saved from harm.

Jesus understands relational challenges, in Mark 3: 31-35 the bible says, *"Then His brothers and His mother came, and standing outside they sent to Him, calling Him. And a multitude was sitting around Him; and they said to Him, "Look, Your mother and Your brothers are outside seeking You." But He answered them, saying, "Who is My mother, or My brothers?" And He looked around in a circle at those who sat about Him, and said, "Here are My mother and My brothers! For whoever does the will of God is My brother and My sister and mother."*

The Bible is clear. We are to honor those in authority over us, including our parents, but not at the risk of being disobedient to the assignment given to us from the Lord.

Dear friend, this is what I believe to be the ultimate challenge: to honor the Lord in our relationships while remaining obedient to His call on our lives. I have seen many spouses and children become angry with God because of a family member who received an assignment from God who was not mentored through this challenge. There is usually one of two common reactions: "God has called me and I must forsake you to answer the call. After all, how can two walk together unless they agree?" or "I will quit the mission to show you that you are more important to me. God will understand." Neither of these reactions is correct. There are no simple answers nor is there a ten-step guide to navigating relationships. You need to have a wise mentor in your life who has success-fully balanced family and ministry to walk alongside you as you attempt to do the same. I thank God for the mentors He has placed in my life, in particular, Pastor Mike Servello Sr. and his son Pastor Mike Servello, Jr. They have successfully maintained healthy family and ministry relationships while growing a thriving church. Pastor Mike Sr. has also been successful in passing the mantle to the next generation of leaders.

Leadership must make room for the next gen-eration of leaders to take the ministry to a new level and "just maybe" even do a better job than we did. Like Saul, many leaders react to the next generation of David's double portion anointing with jealousy, insecurity and fear. God help us, is it any wonder why young people leave churches and take their gifting and anointing to the world? God has given me the privilege of mentoring many gifted young men and women who have received a double portion of anointing for their generation. Several of them had served under a Saul-type leader, becoming wounded, confused and bitter. Thankfully, I was able to be a small part of their lives and witness God restoring them to ministry and fruitfulness. I have been blessed by the sweet presence of Jesus that now emanates from their lives.

Over the years, I have talked to numerous believers that feel called to inner city missions. They have great ideas and exude great passion but when they give it their all and try to move forward, they have little or no success. You will know if a mission is your master when the Lord has not called or anointed you to accomplish something but you continue to try to make something happen in your own strength and ability. In one of my brilliant conversations with God, I told Him that such failure doesn't make Him look good. I love it when He interrupts my foolish chatter and speaks a clear word to me. I sensed His reply, "I have no obligation to anything I have not started. Whatever is started in the flesh has to be maintained and sustained by the flesh."

I have learned so much from one of my great mentors, Pastor Doug Stringer (founder of Somebody Cares America and International). He taught me to identify what the Lord is already doing, what He has already appointed and anointed, then to join Him in serving that cause, because that is where His blessing will be! That is exactly what I have experienced by joining my vision with the ministry to Somebody Cares America/ International. The synergy and blessing I am experiencing today would not be present had I continued to do things the way I was before meeting Pastor Doug.

I know that Christ is the Master of this mission because long after I am gone and my name is forgotten, the ministry will not only survive the challenges of the future, but it will thrive because it is anointed and appointed by God. Not only is it a model for the city of Haverhill and the Merrimack Valley, but it is a model for the Church as a tangible expression of Christ in cities throughout New England.

Chapter Nine

The Good,
the Bad and the Ugly

I f you like wearing rose-colored glasses and want to believe that ministry is full of fun, fame and fortune, I suggest you skip this chapter. I feel it is important to share the complete picture of what ministry entails. I've had to be very selective about what I share in this chapter because of the possibility that it might be very hurtful to some of the people whom these stories are about. Let's begin with the good, and move onto the bad and the ugly later!

About one year after SCNE was birthed, I met Pastor Raffoul Najem, Senior Pastor of Community Christian Fellowship in Lowell, Massachusetts (yes, this is the good part!). A woman I knew named Sonia had invited me to a Sunday service. Although I wasn't thrilled about traveling to Lowell (CCF Lowell is two cities away from the city in which I serve), I decided to go anyway. The first message I heard Pastor Raffoul preach was confirmation of every prophetic word God had given me regarding the church that He was moving me into. The following week, I met with Pastor Raffoul to share the vision and mission of Somebody Cares New England. After I finished sharing my heart and vision, he said, "What can we do to serve you?" I was stunned by his question but found myself answering, "My two most pressing needs are to be licensed and ordained" (upon leaving my former church my credentials would be terminated), and "there is great need for an inner city church plant in Haverhill because most of the local churches are not prepared to disciple the people in that distressed area. Their deep-rooted issues and alternative lifestyles often pose great concern amongst many churches (of which I completely understand)." His immediate response was, "Let's do it." I was shocked that he didn't want me to first serve in his church for a year, submit to a background check, wait for him to call my former pastor to find out the "real reason" I was leaving and meet my family. I will never forget what he said when I asked him why he was so willing and quick to receive, bless and release me in the ministry. His reply was, "I know the Spirit of God and I sense His presence. You are a gift from God to this church. I have been praying for Him to send people like you to help us reach our city."

He then invited me to minister the next four weeks on Wednesday nights to teach the congregation how to be missionaries in their cities.

After much prayer and relationship building and armed with an amazing staff of servant leaders that God had called to work alongside me, we planted Community Christian Fellowship of Haverhill (AKA

"Street Church"). Our mission statement is: "Taking the Love and the Power of Christ to the Streets." Our first two years of services were held in donated space of an Episcopal church on Sunday afternoons. The church we were renting was located on the city block with a reputation for having the highest rate of crime, prostitution and drugs in the city. It was the same block where we had been prayer-walking for the past four years, believing the Lord for transformation. Although we didn't notify the newspapers, a front-page article was written stating that we were the *first church planted in the city of Haverhill to meet the needs of the low-income population*. That was great news to me!

In the first year, were able to bank a majority of the tithes and offerings. By the end of the second year, we were asked to leave the Episcopal church for a number of reasons, including doctrinal differences. God used it to move us to the storefronts on the corner block in Haverhill where we had been praying for transformation.

We were excited yet fearful to have our own place. The work that needed to be done to make the storefronts useful and bring them up to code was overwhelming and the cost of both the rent and utilities was a huge step of faith. In addition, the spiritual dynamics surrounding this particular block were going to be challenging, to say the least. A local newspaper had noted that while most churches were moving out of the city to escape inner city issues, CCF Street Church was moving in, in order to bring transformation to the area. Barney Gallagher in the Eagle Tribune stated, "Somebody Cares organization is transforming the old (1916) block into a community-based style of caring about others. A new chapter is being written in the history of religion in Haverhill."

There were a number of homeless men and women in our church that had made, what we believe to be, sincere decisions to follow Jesus. They would continuously ask us to pray that God would provide them with jobs and housing. Some of them were waiting on SSI, SSDI or unemployment benefits. My heart would ache when I thought about the over- whelming challenges they were facing on a daily basis. When I read Isaiah 58:6-12 I would weep for the poor and homeless. Now, these precious people were coming to our church. We believed God was speaking to us through the Isaiah 58 passage and that He wanted to provide them a home with a struc- tured program of discipleship. We offered classes on finances, nutrition, conflict and anger resolution, and Bible. Part of their training in servanthood involved volunteering four hours per week with Somebody Cares New England.

We had been asking the Lord for the finances to buy a three-story apartment building under renova- tion behind our new location within the same block, but real estate was at an all-time high, and the asking price was way out of our price range. Surprisingly, the couple handling the property offered us the entire house for a reasonable rent. We were so excited to have the opportunity. We moved seven of the men in our church off the streets and six months later, rented another three-unit apartment house, taking in five women, one of them with her young son. Each person was expected to pay $100.00 per week, to cover the cost of *everything,* including the use of washers and dryers in each house. A genuine, biblical family community was beginning to emerge and God's presence was evident in making it all come together. Life was good for everyone.

Approximately five months later, things slowly began to take a turn for the worse. Jobs fell through and SSI and SSDI checks were delayed in coming. We experienced one financial challenge after another. At the end of the first year, all of our financial resources were completely gone. Needless to say, we learned what *not* to do when providing living quarters to those in financial distress. For one, trained residential staff would need to be hired to manage the conflicts and arguments that arose on a daily basis. We also learned that not everyone who knows Jesus is willing to let go of the past and learn new ways. Although the residents had received Jesus, not all of them were willing to crucify their sin nature. This caused a great deal of difficulty and pain for everyone. Providing a stable living environment does not guarantee a better life for people. The spiritual warfare surrounding the lives of these individuals was much more intense than any of us anticipated.

Now for the bad and the ugly part, which I feel is important to share. Some of the people we gave the most time, energy, patience and counsel to started lying and cheating and a few began drinking and using drugs. One person even ended up stealing from the ministry and from their housemates. And in one instance, we had to call the police to help us deal with a mentally unstable resident. It took five policemen, using mace and force, to physically remove him from the property. Often times, as believers we tend to become insular, looking for answers within the four walls of the church. But God's provision comes from various places, including the police, mental health professionals and probation officers.

To say the least, this was a challenging time. A spirit of confusion permeated the atmosphere, as strife and contention became the new household members. Arguing, selfishness and bitterness had to be dealt with on a daily basis. Many evil accusations were made about my staff and the ministry by a couple of the individuals we had helped. Rumors spread through the city like wildfire. It was devastating for everyone. We loved them and thought love would take care of everything. We learned that bad, ugly things sometimes happen, even when you are doing the right thing for the right reasons. At the close of that year, we shut down the housing program and relocated those that remained into housing. The good news is that none of them returned to homelessness!

In his book, "Time to Cross the Jordan," Dr. Doug Stringer does an outstanding job of teaching the biblical truths from the book of Nehemiah. His book has greatly helped me to understand the challenges I have faced as one called by God to restore old waste places and rebuild former foundations.

Nehemiah was a man under authority, and his burden for the well-being of God's people and God's name was his only motivation.

He experienced accusation, confusion, conspiracy, derision, fear, contention, distraction as well as the temptation to react to his circumstances in his flesh. The objective of the opposition was to cripple Nehemiah emotionally, mentally, physically and spiritually, thereby stopping the work of God. The adversary always targets those who are acting on behalf of God's kingdom purpose.

Since moving to our new storefront location, God has added new families, former gangsters, business people, senior citizens and former bikers to the church. Although they differ in age, color and social status, they all have one thing in common: a heart for God and for the city. It is beautiful to watch the Lord minister to them all. Only God can take such a diverse group of people and make them His family.

Chapter Ten

Yah, But...

I don't know about you, but I have a collection of "yah buts." A "yah but" is the part our journey with the Lord in which "stuff happens" that we can't wrap our mind around or reconcile. These "yah buts" can cause a wrestling in our soul, and has great potential to get us stuck - permanently. These bad, ugly things find us even when we are minding our own business and doing the right stuff. Over the years, I've learned how to move ahead in spite of them. I will share with you some of my "yah but" moments in which God has broken through, by giving me revelation from His Word. I will also share some that I have filed away in my "yah but" file cabinet.

One of the "yah buts" I had to wrestle with is death. When I was a new Christian, my husband and I were attending church with a guy we knew from High School. He and his wife had a little girl named Rachel. When Rachel was about eighteen months of age, she died in her crib. When I found out the news, I screamed at God saying, "I thought I could trust you with my children! I will never trust you again, not with my children or anyone else I love." I am so glad He understands the foolish chatter we speak out of fear and anger. In His kindness, God gave me a wonderful dream shortly after Rachel's death. In the dream, I saw her lying dead in her crib in a darkened room. Suddenly, the door opened and an extremely bright light radiated throughout the room. Next, I saw Jesus and was paralyzed by His presence as I watched Him walk to her crib and reach His arms out to her. Rachel opened her eyes and reached out to Jesus as he helped her stand in the crib. She then wraps her arms around His neck, her face beaming with joy. She was so happy to see Him. After cuddling for a few moments, Jesus turned to walk out the door with Rachel. She was dressed in faded, denim jeans and a little, red sweater. I didn't tell anyone about the dream.

Several months later, I helped Rachel's parent's move out of the apartment where she died. The pain made it unbearable for them to live there. As I was unwrapping family pictures one picture in particular caused me to break down in tears. The colored pencil sketch was a picture of Jesus with a little girl that looked like Rachel and she was dressed in faded, denim jeans and a little, red sweater. Rachel was hugging Jesus' neck and they were cuddling. She had the same big smile on her face I had seen in the dream. I tried to hide what was happening to me, but Rachel's mother came into the room and saw me crying. Concerned, she asked me what was wrong so I proceeded to tell her about the dream. Rachel's mother told me that someone had bought that picture several months before Rachel died because it looked so much like her. The day Rachel died, she was wearing faded jeans and a little, red sweater. I told Rachel's mother that God had not only comforted me with the dream, but He used it to reveal to me it that Rachel (whose name means Lamb of God) belonged to Him and she had entered into unspeakable joy and absolute peace; the same peace God desires to give to those who have been separated from her.

Walking through the painful experience of losing Rachel, God has given me the courage to walk through many other tragic losses of children and adults that I have loved deeply. Like Job, I have learned to trust the Lord with the lives of those I love. *"The Lord gives and the Lord takes away, blessed be the name of the Lord."* (Job 1:21). And as David wrote in Psalm 23, *"Yea, though I walk through the valley of the shadow of death I will fear no evil, thy rod and thy staff they comfort me."* The sooner we come to grips with the fact that we are not in control of life or death, the sooner we can let go and trust that our

Heavenly Father has it all under control. Our children and loved ones are on loan to us for a season of time which has been determined in the great book in heaven. Psalm 139:16 says, our days are numbered by the Lord. God understands how hard it is for us to be separated from the ones we love. That is why He sent Jesus to bridge the gap between us, so that we might be reconciled with Him. He crossed over into our world, so that we might cross over into His. I thank God for the cross! One day, we will know the same joy Rachel experienced when we are reunited with the Lord and our loved ones.

Another "yah but" that used to send me into a downward spiral of self pity and despair goes something like this: "If I am doing the right stuff, why don't things turn out the way I had hoped, believed or planned? Why wasn't I getting the results others were getting (or it appeared they were getting)? Why, when I tried so hard, was I ending up disappointed?" Halleluiah, God broke through my foolish chatter yet again! Hebrews 11: 13 says, ...and some having died never seeing the promise knew that there was a greater promise. Some things are appointed to happen *after* we die. Many artists, authors, inventors and missionaries didn't enjoy the fruit of their labors while they were alive. Oftentimes, it is after they passed on, that their work impacted hundreds, thousands or millions of people. Romans 8:17-18 says, *"....if indeed we suffer with Him, that we may also be glorified together. For I consider that the sufferings of this present time are not worthy to be compared with the glory which shall be revealed in us."*

Some of the "yah buts" of which I have yet to receive revelation: How can we say that we know and love Him, yet be so unforgiving to others? How do we manage to judge others harshly and critically, while wanting understanding and mercy for ourselves? When Jesus returns, the Word tells us He is coming back for a church without spot, wrinkle or blemish - how is He ever going to accomplish what looks to be impossible? When is the Lord going to vindicate the injustice of over fifty million innocent babies who have died from abortion? What is He going to do about the corruption of political and church leaders? What about the injustice and cruelty against children by the very parents that gave them life, or the men who father children only to deny them nurture, provision and protection? My only resolve is....but God! Judging from His Word, could it be that He is going to allow great tragedy, famine and darkness for a season in order to perfect those who claim to know Him but deny His Lordship and the power of His Holy Spirit? After all, I Peter 4:17 says, *"For the time has come for judgment to begin at the house of God; and if it begins with us first, what will be the end of those who do not obey the gospel of God?"*

Job is my favorite Bible hero. He endured tremendous suffering, loss, pain and confusion even though he was righteous and did not sin against God or his "comforters". I love what he says at the end of Job 42:25, *"I had heard of you through the hearing of my ears, but now I see you"*. That's what it's all about: seeing Him and being transformed into His likeness through this journey we call life.

Nothing zaps your strength like living in the land of the "yah buts." I used to say, "When I get to heaven, I have a lot of questions for God to answer!" Then God broke through and enlightened me with I John 3:2: *"Beloved, now we are children of God; and it has not yet been revealed what we shall be, but we know that when He is revealed, we shall be like Him, for we shall see Him as He is."* All of the questions that don't get answered while we are on earth won't matter once we see Him. I constantly make the choice to not waste time, energy and thoughts on the things I can't understand so I can give the necessary time, energy and thoughts to the things I can be faithful with now.

My heart breaks for those who refuse to trust God despite the "yah buts," and choose to live in the limbo land of "Nod." My prayer is that the Lord will reveal His goodness to you through a dream, a prophetic word or some other miraculous sign and that, if it doesn't happen, you will choose to be okay with that. My advice to you is the same advice I give myself: in the light of eternity, it really doesn't matter if we know the answers. Take the "yah buts" and put them in the "yah but" file cabinet so you can get on with your life. Your family needs you, the church needs you and the world needs you. You're wasting precious time that could be better spent doing something of value for His kingdom!

Chapter Eleven

He is Good, All the Time

G od rocks my world. When you think you are sacrificing for Him, He has ways of blessing you and it always outweighs anything you can attain on your own. In Chapter Seven, I made reference to a prophetic word I received that God was going to use my husband to help me transition from my former church. Since 1985, I had been praying for the Lord to move us closer to the church we had been attending for over twenty years (it was an hour, round trip). On numerous occasions, I thought I heard the Lord say He was going to build us a house. Sure enough, in

July of 1999, we moved into my dream house. It was absolutely mind blowing. We bought it in the second week of construction, I was able to pick out everything. It was like "moving on up from the east side".

Two years later, my husband Harry suffered a heart attack and needed to be air-lifted by helicopter to Boston for emergency surgery. The doctor told me that had he arrived ten minutes later, I would have had to pick out a stone for him. After returning home, the recovery process revealed that our dream home was just too big maintain. Harry decided it was best to sell the new house and move. I was devastated. This house was a dream that had finally come true. How could Harry and God do this to me? Harry survived an unexpected heart attack and now I was ready to kill him! To say the least, this was definitely one of those "yah but" moments!

Eventually, the Lord reminded me of the prophetic word I had received that He would use my husband to assist me with the transition out of my current church. I praise God for the specific encouragement He had given me that Harry was going to be okay. Harry's heart attack occurred during a time when I was experiencing difficult relational issues surrounding my call to serve in Haverhill and he felt it was a great time for a new beginning for everyone. I am so blessed to have a husband who supports me in my calling. He has sacrificed greatly by releasing me to ministry.

Although I work very hard to balance family and work, it is still a challenge. When I left my full-time, paid position at my former church, it was a financial burden on him because I had been contributing to our household expenses and anything else I needed for the house and myself. I explained to him that I would not get paid to serve as a SCNE missionary. His response was, "I know it's your passion and I support you in your decision." His only concern was that I would have to adjust my lifestyle in order to accommodate my new financial status.

After meeting with the elders to discuss the transition, it was a matter of weeks before our house sold in April 2004. After putting everything in storage, except for the basic necessities, we moved into a tiny five-room apartment over looking the river. I called it my "summer home" on the river.

Looking for a new home in Haverhill, Massachusetts was discouraging. In New Hampshire, you can purchase twice the house for half the money. Everything we looked at within our price range either needed work, was too small or smelled like mold... yada, yada, yada! At one point during our search, I was standing in the tiny, galley kitchen in our small apartment and began to pray, "Lord it is no sacrifice what I have given up. As with Abraham and his son, everything belongs to you. You give and You take away, blessed be the name of the Lord. God, I'm not asking for a big, beautiful house. I just want Your authority and anointing to serve the city you sent me to. You have sent me to open the prison doors and let the oppressed go free, to see deliverance, miracles and transformation manifested in the city streets of

Haverhill so that Your name would be known and glorified!"

In September 2004, we moved into our new, beautiful home. Everyone who comes to visit says the same thing: "I thought your other house was amazing, but this one exceeds it in every way!" The Lord can do miraculous, amazing, incredible things. Not only is our mortgage less, but our taxes are half the price they were in New Hampshire. As it is written in Matthew 19:29, *"I have received one hundred fold in this life!"*

Within the first month of moving into our new home, the newspapers wrote about my recent move to Haverhill, announcing to the whole city that I had been sent to Haverhill on a mission. Shortly after, I was contacted by founding board members of SCNE and very dear friends of mine, Dr. Gene and Sandy Heacock. Gene called me and informed me that, during their recent move to Ohio, he had bought the original seal of Haverhill from the man in western Massachusetts who had made it. Not knowing what I had prayed, Gene said to me, "When I saw it, I knew the Lord wanted you to have it as a reminder that He has given you authority in the city of Haverhill as a sent one." WOW, isn't God good? My life is full of miraculous stories just like this one!

At another time, I had a very specific dream. In the dream, I was a candy stripper in a hospital. My job was to deliver flowers and run errands for the patients. As I approached one room in particular, I saw several medical professionals attempting to calm a lady who was out of control. I stood outside the door listening to her screams for help and wept for her. She was angry, full of rage and exhibited amazing physical strength. After several minutes of trying to physically restrain her, the hospital employees gave her a shot to sedate her. I stood outside the door and continued to weep for her.

After she calmed, the attendants left the room and I went in to talk to her. I couldn't see the features of her face, but I knew from the color of her skin and the sound of her broken English, she was Hispanic.

As she sat on the edge of her bed, exhausted from the fight and numb from the medication, she said to me, "Please give me something for the pain." I told her, "I have no authority to give you medication, but I do have something for you. I wrapped my arms around her and hugged her. Through the open back of her hospital gown, I felt safety pins piercing her back. My heart wrenched in sadness for her. The pain she was suffering must have been so gruesome in order for her to allow someone to do such a thing to her. As my hands touched the wounds on the flesh of her back, I felt compassion and a release of the Lord's love for her. After a few brief moments, I stepped back, not knowing what to expect. She was glowing with a radiant smile of peace and joy. She asked, "What just happened to me? I am no longer in pain and for the first time in my life, I feel love!"

Several months later, while serving at the Drop-In on a Monday holiday, a crazy, Puerto Rican girl named Annette came in ranting and raving, looking for a fight and attention of any kind. She was high on cocaine. For whatever reason, every time she saw me, she would go off saying, "Them loco Christians here again!" Oh my, she was spicy. Her nick name was "firecracker." "Fireworks" (the grand finale) would have been a more appropriate nick name. After several months of loving her and showing her patience and kindness, Annette began to trust me. One day, she opened her heart to receive Christ. When I asked her why she was so aggressive toward the "loco Christians," she answered, "A lot of Christians think they can just walk in here acting like they care about us, only to quit on us a few months later. They don't have any guts. I was testing you to see what you were made of because I had to see if you really cared."

I continued to disciple Annette for about four months until she realized she needed to go to a detox center to get clean and get out of Haverhill. The day I brought her to the detox center, she asked me to pick up the one bag of belongings she had at the shelter. The staff person wouldn't give me the bag without first dumping everything out to make sure she wasn't stealing anything from the shelter. At the very bottom of the bag was a tiny Puerto Rican flag made out of little colored beads and safety pins. As I stood there with the pins in my hand, I had an epiphany: Annette was the crazy, Puerto Rican in my dream and God had healed her pain with His love. WOW, God is so good to let me be a part of His dream to reach people with His love.

The last story I would like to share with you is about Peter. I was familiar with who Peter was. I had seen him on several occasions throughout the city. He was raised in New York City and became a gang member by the time he was thirteen years old. He lived a life of pain in his home as well as on the streets. In an effort to escape the pain of his life, he had begun a journey to Canada, only to end up in Haverhill.

Peter was an alcoholic and a liver transplant recipient. Eventually, he married the love of his life, only to lose her to cancer three years later. Overcome with grief and sorrow, Peter could no longer cope with life. He had become a recluse, sitting in the darkness of his apartment day in and day out. One Sunday morning, he woke up and decided, "This is the day I am going to Plug's Pond to hang myself." He packed a rope in his backpack and began his several mile journey to Plug's Pond to end his life. His travel brought him to the front door of CCF "Street Church," just as Sunday service was starting. Some of the leaders were on the sidewalk greeting people, as Peter was walking by. In Peter's words, "Something gripped my heart and I knew that I needed to go in. As I sat there during the worship and message, I sensed a peace that I have never known before. I knew that I was loved and I wanted to stay here. I had never felt that in church before."

During that service, Michelle, one of my staff, received a prophetic word of encouragement for Peter: "The Lord calls you faithful, you are a faithful man and the Lord is going to bless you for your faithfulness." Based on what I had known of Peter, faithful was not the word that came to my mind when I saw him. He was depressed, disheveled and undone. Thankfully, the Lord sees beyond where we are and knows where we are meant to be. Like the Bible character, Peter, who was like a reed blowing in the wind, Jesus called him a "rock."

Today, Peter is one of the most faithful and dedicated servants of the Somebody Cares Outreach Center and CCF's "Street Church" of Haverhill. His powerful testimony has encouraged many lives. When we are asked to share the vision of Somebody Cares with other churches, we often bring Peter to share his testimony. He has shared his testimony with thousands of people at our annual block parties and he translates for us "white folk" so we can better serve our precious Hispanic community. The Lord has also blessed us with other faithful volunteers Sharon, Marie, Barry, Jim and Don. The daily work of meeting the critical needs of those in the community, could not be done without them.

In an effort to end this chapter with some final words of encouragement, I will share a few details from some of the prophetic words I have received from Pastor Jude Fouquier. A few years ago, at a Generation Conference with over a thousand attendees, Pastor Jude belted out, "Marlene Yeo, are you here? The Lord is giving you an anointing of breakthrough for the mentally ill. He is going to use you to set the captives free and to heal their minds." On another occasion, Pastor Jude exhorted that I would eventually have my own television show. Through an amazing series of events (yet another story!), we have been in production on the local cable television channel since April of 2007. On the show, I have had the opportunity of hosting numerous people who have shared incredible testimonies of what the Lord has done in their lives through Somebody Cares. Peter and Sharon were guests on the show and their story has touched thousands of lives. Sharon was the youngest child to be admitted to the Boston Children's Hospital due to a nervous breakdown. When Sharon gave her heart to the Lord, she finally found love and acceptance and the Lord healed her. Her doctor has since told her that she no longer needs to be on her psych medication. She has been declared emotionally healthy and mentally sound! People from all walks of life have told me how much they love the show and that they are glad we are able to share what Somebody Cares is doing in the city. You can catch the monthly show online at: www.haverhillcommunitytv.org.

Chapter Twelve

To Be Continued...

I can hardly wait to see what the future holds for both Somebody Cares New England and CCF "Street Church." We have built strong relationships with over eighteen city agencies, organizations and churches serving the population of people that we are called to serve. Recently, I requested to speak before the Haverhill City Council on a building code issue. While there, I received commendations from many city councilmen, with special words of praise from a former mayor and a detective. They informed me that, since SCNE and CCF moved onto the city block, formerly referred to as "Bannon's Spa," the block is cleaner, the crime rate has dropped, and some of the former substance abusers are now giving back to the community through the ministry. The detective said, "There are many supporters of your ministry here tonight, and I would like the cameramen to get it on the TV cameras." He went on to say, "I can personally attest to the transformation of the lives of some of the people who are here tonight. The city appreciates all that you are doing to help the citizens of Haverhill. Keep up the good work."

During the time of writing of this book, we are praying for a miracle that the Lord will make it possible for us to purchase the first church built in the city of Haverhill. It is located directly across the street from City Hall (how cool is that?). It has ample parking, green space, an amazing kitchen, a dining hall with a stage, and a great sanctuary. It has been for sale for almost three years. The asking price is above our price range, but we are preparing to make an offer to purchase it at the assessed valued once we have saved a down payment of twenty percent. We believe it is a perfect match for CCF, the "first church" planted in the city of Haverhill for those in distress.

When Pastor Mike Servello, Sr. came to preach at the launching service for CCF Haverhill, he said to me, "Marlene, because you are willing to care for the ones nobody wants, God is going to bring you the ones everybody wants." I know the Lord has only just begun to do what He desires in Haverhill, Massachusetts, the Merrimack Valley and New England. I am so grateful to God for allowing an ordinary person like me to partner with Him in bringing about His dream for this region.

Where is God on Tuesday? I'll tell you where He is. He is seated on the throne, far above all rulers, principalities and powers, looking for the weak, foolish ones on the earth through whom He can show Himself strong. His thoughts for you are good, not evil, and He desires to bless you with a bright future full of hope (Jeremiah 29:11).

Are you one of the weak, foolish ones wanting God to use you to demonstrate His awesome love and power? Does your heart yearn for something more than the traditional routine of Christianity? For those of you who feel called to live a *lifestyle* of sharing the gospel with "not yet" believers, maybe God is calling you to be a part of a global prayer compassion movement that is "bigger than yourself." If you would like more information about Somebody Cares and CCF "Street Church," please see our contact information below.

SCNE/ CCF

P.O. Box 5032

Haverhill, MA 01835

CCF Phone: (978) 912-7616

SCNE Phone: (978) 912-7626

E-mail: office@somebodycaresne.org

www.CCFStreetChurch.org

www.SomebodyCaresNE.org

www.SomebodyCares.org